CONTENTS

Look out for the underlined words in this book, they are explained in the glossary on page 24.

©2016
Book Life
King's Lynn
Norfolk PE30 4LS

ISBN: 978-1-910512-43-2

Written by:
Gemma McMullen

Edited by:
Harriet Brundle

Designed by:
Matt Rumbelow & Ian McMullen

A catalogue record for this book is available from the British Library.

WHAT IS MEAT AND FISH?

Meats are foods from animals that we eat. Fish and eggs are also animal products.

Meat and fish are eaten as an important part of our diets.

Meat, fish, eggs, beans and nuts are all foods high in <u>protein</u>.

WHAT IS PROTEIN?

Our bodies need protein from meat and other sources to make them grow. Protein helps the body to repair itself.

Protein should be eaten as part of most of our meals as it gives us energy.

Egg on Toast

Prawn Salad

Roast Dinner

MEAT

Meat includes lamb, beef, pork and <u>poultry</u>, such as chicken and turkey. These meats are made into a variety of products.

Most meats need to be cooked before they are eaten. It is especially important to cook poultry products well. Uncooked poultry can make us unwell.

Cooked

Raw

9

MEAT PRODUCTS

Meat is used in a variety of ways. Pork can be used as a joint, put into sausages or made into ham and bacon.

Sausages

Kidney Pie

Bacon

Meat also includes the organs of animals, such as kidneys.

Meat is also put with other ingredients to make tasty dishes.

Lasagne

11

FISH

There are hundreds of species of fish, some of which are eaten by humans. Common foods include cod, tuna, haddock and salmon.

Seafood and shellfish such as squid, crabs and mussels also contain protein.

Seafood is usually eaten cooked, although Japanese sushi is eaten raw.

FISH PRODUCTS

Fish can be used in a variety of ways. It can be baked or fried and is also put with other ingredients to make delicious meals.

Salmon en Croute

Paella

Cooked fish can be enjoyed warm or cold with a salad or in a sandwich.

Tuna Sandwich

WHERE DO WE GET MEAT AND FISH FROM?

The animals used for meat are raised on special farms. Some meat gets sent to factories to be put into food products. The rest goes to shops and supermarkets.

Some fish are farmed, others are caught from the sea using large nets.

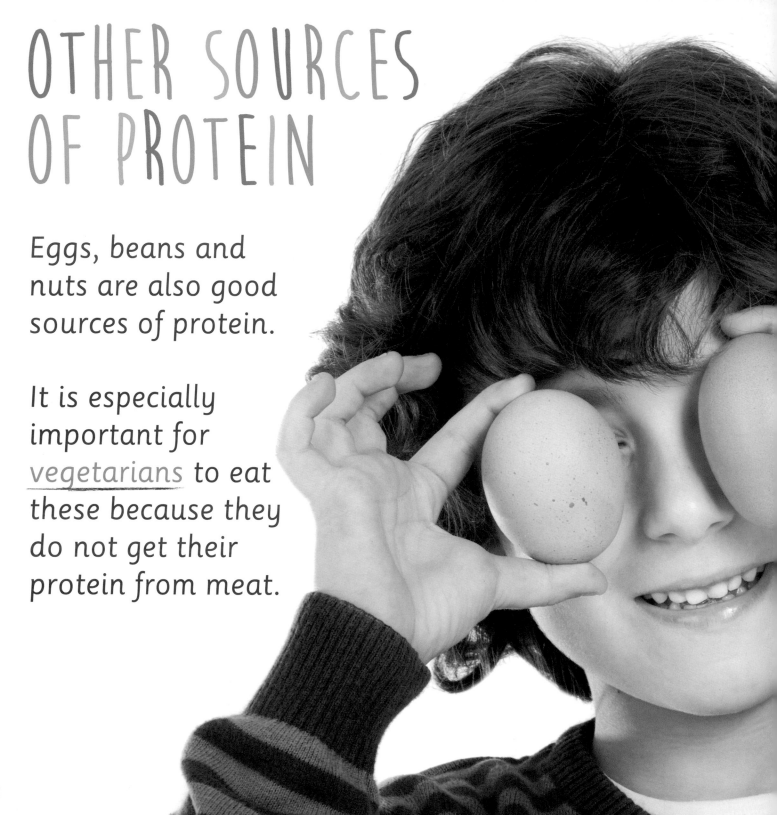

OTHER SOURCES OF PROTEIN

Eggs, beans and nuts are also good sources of protein.

It is especially important for vegetarians to eat these because they do not get their protein from meat.

Eggs come from birds. Beans and nuts come from plants.

HEALTHY PROTEINS

Eating protein helps to keep our bodies healthy. Some foods containing protein are more healthy than others.

Some meat contains a lot of fat. We should try not to eat these foods too often.

21

FOODY FACTS!

Insects contain high levels of protein.

Our muscles and organs are mostly made of protein.

GLOSSARY

factories
buildings where things are made

ingredients
things put together to make
a mixture

poultry
birds raised for meat and eggs

protein
substances in our bodies which
keep us healthy

vegetarians
persons who do not eat meat

INDEX

PHOTO CREDITS